Death Grief Grace

A Memoir of Healing

Sandra VandenBrink

Chapbook Press

Schuler Books

2660 28th Street SE

Grand Rapids, MI 49512

(616) 942-7330

www.schulerbooks.com

Death Grief Grace

ISBN 13: 978196619211

Library of Congress Control Number: 2025906222

Printed in the United States by Chapbook Press.

In the book, *Death Grief Grace*, the author, Sandra VandenBrink draws the reader beside her on a journey through the valley of the shadow of death. By inviting the reader to accompany her, Sandra VandenBrink allows one to simultaneously immerse themselves in loss and experience the healing she discovered through the illness and passing of her beloved husband.

Although I teared-up several times, for example, with the singing of the hymn, "We Plow the Fields and Scatter," the book strikes the right balance between pain, sorrow, and beautiful life-affirming insights. In a crowded genre of publications on grief, most volumes are a drudgery to finish. This book is unique. Never overwhelmed with the darkness of death, each chapter brings a glimmer of light, compassion, and relief from the universal tribulation all must endure on the "terra firma". The ebb and flow of difficult and sweet memories fill each chapter. With the conclusion of each section the author shares her profound understanding of the meaning one can explore by sitting with one's emotions.

Sandra VandenBrink is a great storyteller. The author weaves her lived experiences into an interesting, heartwarming reflection on relationships, faith, hope and love. Her words paint pictures which stimulate the 'senses' of the reader. At times, I inhaled the rich poignant 'scent' which accompanies the precious experiences of our lives i.e. walking with a companion on the beach, holding hands with a lover, sitting beside a partner during their final days on earth or watching a loved-one quietly slip away from this side of life. If one is willing to learn and grow from pain and loss, then, walk with Sandra VandenBrink and allow her to help guide your pathway forward. I highly recommend the memoir: *Death Grief Grace*.

—Steve Dieleman, Master Certified Health Education Specialist (MCHES) Certified Prevention Consultant (CPC) Youth Mental Health First Aid Instructor, Retired. Editor & Artist. *Our Very Small & Violent Children*, Co-Author.

Contents

Preface

Are we ever truly prepared for the death of a loved one? Even when we try to live each day as if it might be our last, we tend to deny death's inevitability—as if it couldn't happen to us or those we love.

For those who care for someone lingering in that liminal space between life and death, awareness of mortality becomes a constant companion. Yet does this awareness make the final moment any easier? I'm not certain. My own experience with sudden loss came when my father died at the age of 53 from a massive heart attack, leaving my mother a widow at just 50.

I remember driving to her home the night of his death. She sat on the couch in her fluffy robe, having just showered after returning from the hospital. The sight jarred me—my mother, always so well put together with carefully applied makeup and styled hair, now stripped of all pretense by grief. In that moment of devastation, her appearance no longer mattered. I wonder now if she had ever truly considered the possibility of becoming a widow so young, left alone to raise one child still at home.

My father had lived precariously—a heavy smoker who paid little attention to his diet. Exercise was foreign to him, and his attempt at weight management followed a familiar pattern of loss and regain. Had my mother ever imagined she would be left alone at 50, a stay-at-home mom with limited job prospects? Looking back 50 years later, I shudder. How did she manage? How does anyone survive the loss of a spouse, a child, or a partner—someone so deeply woven into the fabric of our lives?

Many of us find ourselves in territory we never imagined we would have to navigate. Experts tell us that losing a close loved one changes us fundamentally—even alters our brain chemistry. I believe this to be true. Reflecting on my own grief journey—from the days of caregiving through the moment of death, and the subsequent days, weeks, months and years—I recognize profound changes in myself. Most have been transformative: I've grown stronger, wiser, and more resilient. Above all, my capacity for empathy has expanded, embracing not just those who grieve, but anyone struggling with life's challenges. My heart has grown larger, making room for more love, patience, and understanding.

Through my writing, I hope to share this journey of death, grief, and grace. I want to encourage others walking this path to recognize the profound wisdom and unexpected blessings that can emerge from an experience none of us would choose. I view the grief process as gathering the fragments of a shattered life and weaving them into something meaningful—something that might light the way for others.

Frederick Buechner, whose father died by suicide when Fred was a young boy, often wrote about the pain of that devastating loss. As both pastor and writer, he chose to redeem this painful experience by becoming what he called "a good steward of his pain." This poses a vital question for all who face loss and grief: How can we transform our pain into something beneficial for ourselves and others? How do we avoid becoming trapped in the depths of sorrow?

I believe we have both a duty and a choice to gather the scattered pieces of our lives and continue living. This, I'm certain, is what our loved ones would want for us. A verse from Deuteronomy 30:19 has become my touchstone:

> Today I have given you the choice between life and death, between blessings and curses. Now I call on heaven and earth to witness the choice you make. Oh, that you would choose life, so that you and your descendants might live.

As I walk this grief journey, I have decided to choose life, and with God's help, I shall persist.

Trevor and I at the Humber Bridge the year we walked
across England following the Hadrian's Wall Walk.

"One day you will tell your story of how you've overcome, and it will become part of someone else's survival guide."

Brené Brown

"In Our End Is Our Beginning" – T.S. Eliot

I stepped through the front door with my black Lab, Lucy, after completing our daily walk in Barstow Woods: I sensed an unmistakable presence in the house. The atmosphere felt heavy, though not dark or foreboding. Our beloved Hospice home health aide, Kathy, was there, bringing her usual spirit of kindness and gentleness. But something had shifted—I could feel it. My husband, who had been ill for many years and bedbound for the past year requiring 24-hour care, was breathing his last breaths. Death was in the house, taking hold of him, yet I felt no fear as God's loving presence enveloped us.

I approached my husband's bed. Kathy had carefully washed and shaved him, dressing his limp, thin body in his favorite University of Michigan shirt. Perhaps she knew something about this day that I didn't. We had all known this day would come—this death day—though there had been many times before when death seemed imminent. Today felt different. I had learned that experienced Hospice staff possess a certain knowing. While families are taught the signs and symptoms of dying — shallow breathing, cold extremities, death rattle, refusing food and water—Hospice workers seem to possess an intuition that extends beyond the obvious. They sense things, perhaps through some form of extra sensory perception. It seemed fitting, then, that Kathy had chosen Trevor's favorite shirt for this day.

Standing at his bedside, I felt apprehensive and sad, dreading what I knew was coming. Trevor briefly opened his eyes as I spoke to him, my words attempting to calm both his fears and my own. I expressed my love and gratitude for our years of companionship, for all the joys our family had shared. I assured him that we would be all right, that he could leave when he felt ready. He slowly turned his head away, and his breathing ceased.

I laid my head on his now-silent chest and wept, as I weep now recounting that day. The experience feels mystical, surreal—almost an out-of-body experience for me, and truly one for Trevor. His physical body had stopped working, his spirit quietly departing. When his spirit left his body, sorrow overwhelmed me. The tears flowed gently, unlike the keening wails that often accompany sudden death. I believe a sudden death would have been far more difficult to bear.

God granted me the gift of time—months, even years, to prepare for this day. Through years of his slow decline and months of caregiving, I gradually awakened to the reality that one day I would be alone. I received two profound gifts: God's grace, which enabled me to care for Trevor with gentleness and patience, and God's love, which allowed me to love Trevor beyond human understanding.

Trevor's passing brought both deep sorrow and profound relief, accompanied by a touch of guilt for feeling that relief. Yet knowing that inside his lovely, intelligent, funny, and wise brain lay a tumor too large and intricately entangled to remove, I found solace in the end of his suffering. He was finally free from the physical body that had failed him, trapped him.

The doctors had explained that attempting to remove the tumor would likely worsen his quality of life without extending it. The tumor grew slowly, first diagnosed in 2007 when Trevor experienced numbness and tingling in his forehead. The doctors identified the tumor as a meningioma, a nonmalignant tumor of the brain meninges. The diagnosis came with both good and bad news: while noncancerous and slow-growing, the tumor was massive, impinging on areas of his brain controlling speech, cognition, and bodily functions. They warned it might lead to seizures and paralysis. In the end, it did all of that. Yet remarkably, two things endured: his quirky British sense of humor and the twinkle in his eyes.

Death and dying are universal experiences, yet deeply personal and unique. Just as no two people are exactly alike, no two deaths are identical. Some pass quietly in their sleep, others through traumatic events—massive heart attacks, strokes, or fatal accidents. Some, like Trevor, experience a long, slow decline. No manner of death proves easier for the survivor than another. The variables are countless, yet all death leads to enormous heartbreak, deep loss, and disorientation.

My grief story echoes those of others who have lost spouses of many years, yet every story—and every effort to rebuild life after such a profound change—remains unique. In sharing my story of death, grief, and grace, I hope to help others understand and grow from their own grief experiences. Death and grief present perhaps the most challenging events we must face; yet hope, goodness, blessing, and grace await those willing to wrestle with deep sorrow and learn to live without their loved one's physical presence.

Sharing my story aids my healing, compelling me to reflect on this difficult period with sadness, resolve, and a powerful reminder of my fortitude. Through writing and reflection, I've come to recognize the bravery and compassion I demonstrated in the face of death and grief. While the early days after loss shroud us in confusion and numbness, as time passes, we can indeed "see the goodness of the Lord in the land of the living" (Psalm 27).

Visits occurred in every season.

So much love between Trevor and his children

A Good Death

Finding Grace In Goodbye

Death comes to us all like seasons—sometimes with winter's sudden frost, other times like autumn's gradual turning of leaves. Yet we can approach it with intention, treating each sunrise as a gift unwrapped, each sunset as a gentle reminder of our mortality. Through this mindful approach, death transforms from a feared stranger into a sacred transition, like twilight melting into starlight.

My husband's death, while carving deep valleys of grief in my heart, carried its own particular grace. During his 15 months in Hospice care, he became an alchemist of moments, turning ordinary days into gold. His eyes still sparkled with mischief as he nicknamed the Hospice workers "dead enders." His Yorkshire accent grew stronger as he serenaded his favorite caregiver with old pub songs from his youth, painting vivid pictures of cobblestone streets, rugby games, and warm ales from his younger days.

The Covid pandemic draped additional shadows across our path, reducing visits to window-side gatherings beside his hospital bed. Yet even this limitation birthed unexpected joy—our children and grandchildren transformed the backyard into an impromptu stadium, performing elaborate sports routines just to make him smile. Each visit concluded with our family's slightly off-key but heartfelt rendition of "God Save the Queen," their voices carrying across the window screen barrier. Through spring's tender blossoms, summer's heavy heat, autumn's painted leaves, and winter's crystalline chill, these window serenades became our family's anthem of resilience, our chorus of undying love.

Though I harbor no fondness for death—who among us does?—I've learned it needn't wear the mask of terror. There are ways to make dying as gentle as dusk, as meaningful as a well-worn love letter. While I navigate the landscape of grief, taking each day like steps on an unfamiliar path, I can say with quiet certainty that my husband's death was good. He died as he lived—on his own terms, wrapped in a tapestry of love, his final months teaching us all about the art of leaving gracefully, about finding light even in life's deepest shadows.

Because of the Lord's great love we are not consumed, for his compassions never fail. They are new every morning; great is God's faithfulness. (Lamentation 3:22-23).

"We humans (especially in the West) suffer from a neurotic anxiety about death. In fact, we are absolutely enslaved to that fear, we insulate ourselves from it through distractions, entertainments, and comforts."

Peter Enns

"'Remember your creator in the days of your youth,' as in keep in mind where this journey is ending up so you're not surprised when the day comes. The Psalmist asks God, 'teach us to number our days that we may gain a wise heart.' God's sentence of Adam, 'you are dust and to dust you shall return,' is part of some Christian liturgies, as is Job's acceptance of death when he said, 'Naked I came from my mother's womb and naked shall I return there.'"

Peter Enns

"Death is a return to whence we came. I happen to be one of those people who believes that consciousness is immaterial – it continues after our bodies expire. Accepting death in that respect has made a huge difference to me."

Peter Enns

From Substack "We're All Going to Die, Yay Universe!"

Through the window visit by my daughter Chloe,
son-in-law JT, and grandson Avery

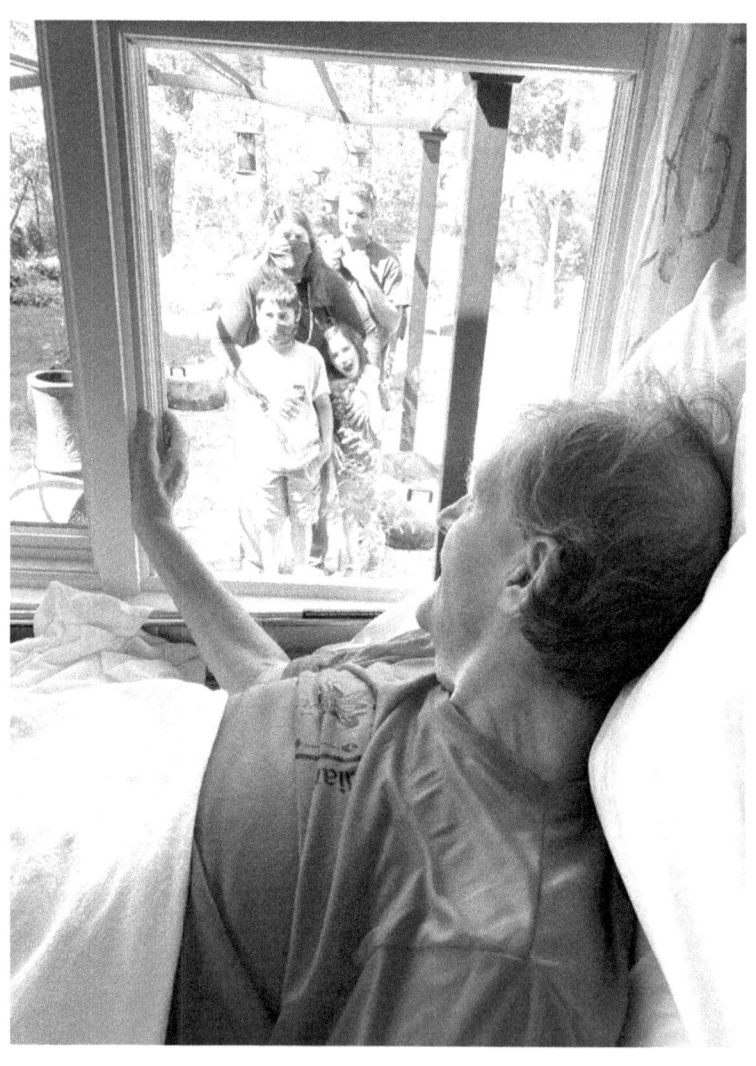

Daughter Dianne and family visited in every season.

Healing on the Isle of Man

The Isle of Man appeared through my rain-streaked windshield like a dark silhouette against the night sky. Six months after Trevor's death, I had come to this unfamiliar place as a deliberate detour from my journey back to Yorkshire to visit his sisters. Something in me knew I needed neutral ground – a place unmarked by memory – before facing the landscape of our shared past.

My late-night arrival set the tone for what would become a transformative stay. Lost in the darkness, I texted my B&B hosts for help. Minutes later, I found my way guided by their elderly hostess, standing in the pouring rain in her pajamas and raincoat, cheerfully waving a full-size Isle of Man flag. The unexpected welcome – this willingness to stand in the storm for a stranger – touched something deep within my grief-weary heart.

That Sunday, when my hostess offered to accompany me to the local church's Harvest Festival, I accepted without realizing I was walking into a moment that would crack open my carefully maintained composure.

Harvest Festival Sunday is an annual tradition in England celebrated at every church and school. The small but ancient stone church was the backdrop for an exquisite offering of seasonal vegetables, fruits, flowers, home-canned goods, and lovely baked pies and cakes that members had contributed to the stunning display on the altar. This was to be a celebration of gratitude for the abundant harvest. The food was a presentation of God's bounty in the harvest.

The church was full for this important annual service of gratitude and thanksgiving, and the children stood to recite their poems about the season. The enormous pipe organ was in full resonance.

I leaned over and whispered to my hostess, "If we have to sing, 'We Plow the Fields and Scatter,' I know I'll start crying." Unsurprisingly, because this is THE traditional harvest hymn, the tears began to flow as the organ played the introduction.

> We plow the fields and scatter the good seed on the land, but it is fed and watered by God's almighty hand. All good gifts around us are sent from heaven above. So, thank the Lord, oh thank the Lord for all his boundless love.

As the tears flowed freely in that stone church, surrounded by the bounty of harvest, memories of Trevor's final months during Covid emerged with startling clarity. The hymn that had just undone me – "We Plow the Fields and Scatter" – had been more than just his favorite. It had been his connection to his roots, to the Yorkshire soil he had worked alongside his father. Now, in this moment of release, I could finally look back at those isolated months of caring for him with new understanding.

Today, emerging from that season of loss, I find myself in my own unexpected harvest time. The seeds of grief, watered by tears in that island church, have slowly begun to yield something new. Like the farmers in Trevor's beloved hymn, I've learned that growth comes not just from our own efforts, but from forces beyond our control – forces that feed and water what we plant.

In this gradual awakening to new life, I'm learning to trust the process of growth itself. The past nourishes rather than haunts me now. Each day, I witness small shoots of possibility emerging from the rich soil of experience. As Julian of Norwich reflected from her own valley of transformation, "All shall be well, and all shall be well, and all manner of things shall be well." In my own heart, watching my careful plantings begin to flourish, I'm starting to understand the deep truth in her words.

The Isle of Man

"I resolved not to disown my grief, but to seek to own it redemptively—own it in such a way that might bring about some good."

Nicholas Wolterstorff

Grief Walking

On a cold, frosty, late-March morning, I laced up my boots, loaded my black Lab, Lucy into the car, and headed for the park. Walking became a healing habit for me in those days of Covid and caregiving. My husband, Trevor, had been in decline for months, years really. As a former hospice chaplain and end of life doula, I recognized the familiar signs of approaching death, yet nothing truly prepares you for watching a loved one fade.

Being a caregiver drains both body and spirit. A terminal diagnosis leaves little room for hope while demanding everything from you. Looking back now, three years later, I can only attribute my strength to God's divine presence. I never considered myself particularly strong or courageous, especially regarding medical care. While I admired nurses and home health aides who confidently provide the most intimate care, I approached each task tentatively, meticulously noting every instruction and change in Trevor's condition. Yet something deeper than my own capabilities carried me through.

Each day presented new challenges that required drawing from that deep spiritual well. Prayer became my lifeline. And so did walking. That chilly day in late March marked the end of my caregiving journey. Trevor had died two mornings before, and though the Hospice nurse offered to call the funeral home immediately, I wasn't ready. I wanted him to stay home another day, allowing our children and grandchildren time for their final goodbyes.

That evening, our family gathered around a campfire outside Trevor's window. We wept, laughed, sang songs, and shared stories. My son-in-law read a poem he'd written about Trevor, who lay peacefully in his beloved University of Michigan attire, covered by a Union Jack blanket—a gift from his special caregiver, Kathy

After the funeral home's unceremonious "removal" the next morning, I found myself adrift in grief's vast ocean. But I discovered my anchor in walking —what I now call grief walking, or as some say, prayer walking. Though I'd never been particularly athletic, during Covid, my only escape during the caregivers' visits had been walking Lucy through Barstow Woods. After Trevor's death, we kept

walking along beaches, through forests, in the arboretum—
anywhere nature offered solace.

With each step, healing began. Walking became a
powerful metaphor for life's journey through grief and
challenge. Though physically alone except for faithful
Lucy, I felt embraced by God's creation—the whispering
trees, lapping waves, blooming wildflowers, and skittering
squirrels. Each season brought its gifts: summer's verdant
canopy, autumn's painted leaves, winter's pristine snow,
and spring's persistent renewal.

The physical and spiritual benefits of walking are well
documented. Beyond the endorphins that boost our mood,
walking offers a moving meditation—space for tears,
reflection, and prayer. In my year of grief walking, Lucy
became both companion and bridge to my life with Trevor.
Often, an old hymn or meaningful quote would surface,
becoming that day's meditation.

Through my time of grief, I learned to breathe deeply, lace up my walking shoes, and embark on a journey toward healing. As Søren Kierkegaard wrote:

> Above all, do not lose your desire to walk. Every day, I walk myself into a state of well-being and walk away from every illness. I have walked myself into my best thoughts, and I know of no thought so burdensome that one cannot walk away from it.

On the beach with Lucy.

Lake Huron, Port Austin, Michigan

Snow Walking

That year
      that year of holy grief
I walked every day
      Not by choice
      by compulsion

In the snow
      the driving snow
      wet snow
         piercing snow

My tears melded
      into the cold dampness,
         bone chilling, face numbing
I wanted those tears and flakes
      to become
         one with my suffering

My grief took
      physical form
to keep me from
      going numb
grief numbness
      survival numbness

I needed the
      freezing,
         the feeling, the pain
to remind me

I am alive

S. VandenBrink

Lucy, the Dog Who Healed Us

A Story of Second Chances and Unconditional Love

The day we met Lucy, I had no idea this traumatized rescue dog would become our family's guardian angel. She sat in the corner of that ramshackle farmhouse, her deep brown eyes carrying shadows of her troubled past, yet still somehow offering a glimmer of hope. Her black fur, despite her rough history, gleamed with an inner light that seemed to whisper of resilience and the possibility of new beginnings.

Lucy's bushy tail would wag endlessly when she greeted someone new, or especially when offered a treat. She had a cheeky way about her—head slightly tilted, ears perked forward—and would do anything for a morsel. She charmed people not just with her plaintive eyes and velvety soft fur, but with a gentle spirit that had somehow survived years of neglect.

Our journey to Lucy began after some fairly tense family negotiations. Our previous dog had died several months earlier, and while it felt like the right time to find a new companion, we insisted it had to be the "perfect" one. Through word of mouth, we learned of a woman who rescued dogs and gave them temporary homes until they could be placed permanently. She wasn't a proper kennel or Humane Society, just a kind, animal-loving soul who couldn't bear to see creatures suffer.

Trevor and I drove out into the countryside one autumn afternoon, the trees aflame with fall colors, to meet this compassionate dog rescuer. Down a dusty, old, unpaved road, we found a rather shabby farmhouse with peeling paint, tall grass, and abandoned farm equipment scattered like forgotten toys. The entrance required careful navigation of rotting, sagging porch boards that creaked ominously under our feet. We entered what was probably called a mudroom, though "mud museum" might have been more accurate—boots, shoes, coats, and hats, all wearing layers of dried earth like badges of honor. Inside, we discovered a bustling menagerie: parrots that squawked hello, cats that wound between our legs, dogs of various sizes and breeds that sniffed us curiously. And there, in a quiet corner, sat Lucy.

"This is Lucy," the lady said softly, motioning toward her. "She's available and such a sweet dog, but she's had a rough go of it." We approached slowly, and Lucy's response told her story—gentle but cautious, hopeful but not trusting, her tail offering a tentative wave like a white flag of truce. She was about four years old, a black Lab mixed with what seemed to be border collie, given her intelligent eyes and graceful build.

The rescue lady's next words should have been a warning: "She was rescued from a family of drug users who would leave her alone for days without food or water. She has separation anxiety—doesn't like being left alone." She said it matter-of-factly, but the implications were enormous. My husband had recently been diagnosed with a brain tumor, and I knew there would be countless medical appointments ahead. Who would stay with a dog who couldn't bear solitude?

But Trevor, perhaps seeing something of himself in Lucy's vulnerability, said simply, "We can handle it. She's perfect."

Looking back, I realize he understood something I didn't–that sometimes our greatest challenges become our greatest gifts.

The first few months tested our commitment severely. Lucy's separation anxiety wasn't just nervousness—it was pure panic. She bent metal crate bars with her teeth, shredded wooden door frames, and turned furniture into sawdust. Even medication from the veterinarian only left her bumping into walls, her anxiety now clouded by sedation but not cured. We hired a "dog whisperer" who gave us rules about furniture and beds (which we promptly ignored) and advised against crate training (which we gratefully abandoned).

We couldn't have known then how crucial this bond would become. When Trevor's condition worsened and he became bedridden, Lucy transformed from being our responsibility to being our rock. She seemed to understand instinctively what was needed—quiet companionship, unwavering presence, and pure, unconditional love. I would arrange a chair next to Trevor's hospital bed, and Lucy would settle in for hours, keeping watch as her presence provided comfort that no medicine would match.

The rhythm of our days changed, Lucy adapted to shorter walks, seemed to know when Trevor needed rest, and became expertly attuned to our emotional states. She who had known such trauma in her early life now become our healer, teaching us that love could flourish even in the shadow of loss.

After Trevor died, Lucy became my lifeline. She got me up each morning when I might have stayed in bed, coaxed me out for walks when I might have isolated myself, and provided warm presence during long, lonely nights. She would rest her head on my lap when I cried, her eyes reflecting a deep understanding that only another soul who had known loss could offer. Together, we created new routines—morning walks in the arboretum where the changing seasons marked time's passage, afternoon visits to the dog park where her playful spirit gradually reawakened my own, and quiet evenings where her steady breathing reminded me I wasn't alone.

As Lucy aged, our roles gradually reversed. Her once-black face turned white, her confident stride became a careful shuffle, and her bright eyes clouded with blindness. The dog who once hiked five miles with ease now tired after one, and nighttime became challenging as she navigated our home in darkness, sometimes crying out in confusion. Yet even then, her loving heart never dimmed.

Three years after Trevor's death, I had to make the heartbreaking decision to let Lucy go. As I held her for that final day, crying into her still-soft fur, I thanked her for being the unexpected angel who had carried us through our darkest days. She had taught us that healing often comes from the most unexpected sources, that damaged hearts have the greatest capacity for love, and that sometimes the ones who need saving end up saving us.

Lucy's story reminds us that perfect love doesn't require a perfect past. Sometimes, the most wounded souls become the most gifted healers, and in saving another, we often save ourselves. She came to us as a dog who needed healing and left us as the dog who healed us.

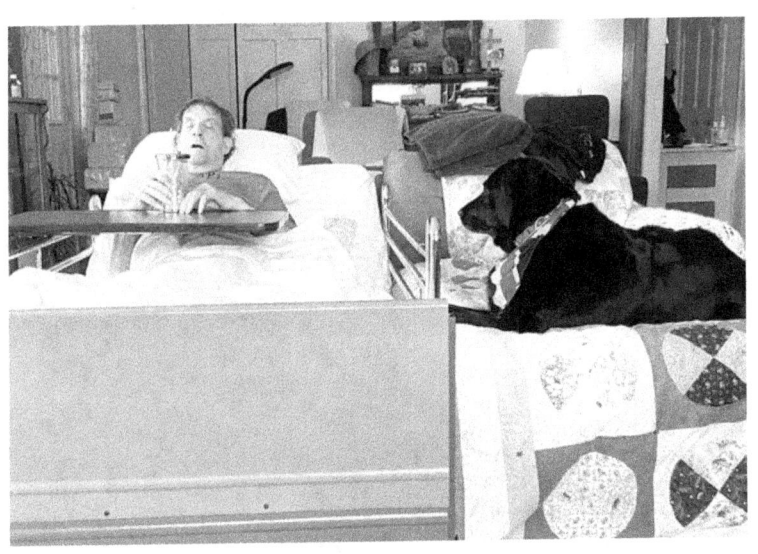

Through the window visit by son Robert

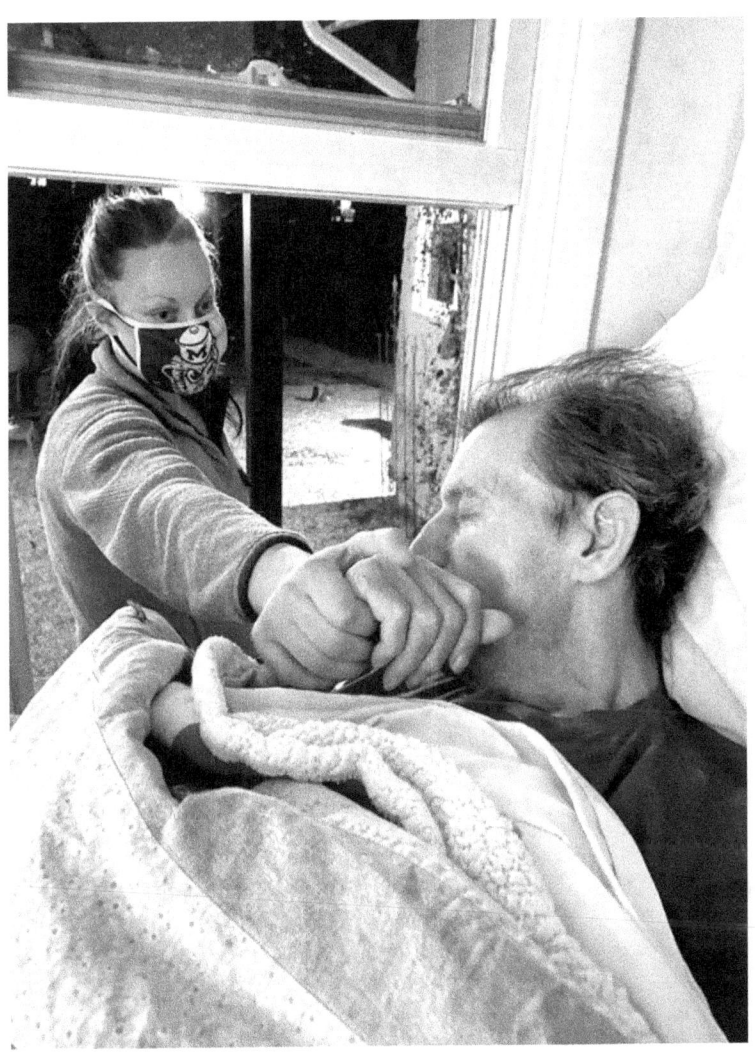

Chloe visited her Dad every day. They always sang together.

Campfires and games in the backyard

Grief Triggers

I was walking tentatively on a half-melted trail in the New Hampshire mountains when I suddenly experienced what I have come to refer to as a "grief trigger." For nearly four years, I've been coping with and processing the loss of my dear husband, Trevor. I had adopted the mantra, "one foot in front of the other, one step at a time," as I literally and figuratively walked my way through the most difficult period of my life. In the early days of grief, I walked every day, and it proved to be a healing balm. But recently, through a series of difficult life events, my walking practice has become irregular. I miss its constancy and the sense of well-being it gave me.

Yesterday, as I walked with my daughter, her husband, and my lively young grandson on the mountain trails of New Hampshire, I experienced what you might call déjà vu. As I carefully walked down a slight incline, my grandson said, "Meema, when you go downhill, lean back, it will help with your balance." Such kind and thoughtful words from a 13 year-old boy who has outpaced his meema in every aspect of high-tech knowledge, and who probably sees me as the greatest example of anachronism that has ever existed.

Two generations separate us. I wrote a book about my life as a gift to him. I doubt he's read it, but maybe when he's my age he'll discover that we didn't have computers until I was well into adulthood. Girls were required to wear dresses to school—no jeans or trousers, and absolutely nothing revealing. These were the 1950s and 1960s, over 70 years ago. This must seem like ancient history to him. The speed of change in the past 60 years has been mind-blowing.

Into this fast-paced world of video games and instant information, I come for a visit to enjoy the slow pace of walking in the woods, appreciating the simplicity of trees and quiet streams, ponds much like Walden Pond. The life of my childhood must feel strangely unfamiliar and quaint to my grandson. I doubt he can imagine lying on your back in the grass with girlfriends, looking up at clouds and imagining animals or angels in their shapes, with no time constraints and lots of giggles. What else was there to do when school was out? Imagination was the palette with which we painted the canvas of shapes and beings that didn't exist in our small, west-central Indiana town.

But I appreciate that my grandson still enjoys the outdoors—the woods, the mountains, even the half-frozen pond he dared venture onto. And in that moment of brief kindness, when he instructed me on how to walk down hills and mountain paths, he triggered something in me.

Nearly 15 years ago, Trevor and I decided to walk across England on the Hadrian's Wall path, about 116 miles. By then, Trevor was already three years past the diagnosis of the nonmalignant, slow-growing brain tumor that made itself apparent in 2007 when he woke up with a tingling in his forehead. We received the diagnosis from a kindly, nearly retired neurologist who said there was good news and bad news: Trevor had a brain tumor, but it was slow-growing and nonmalignant. He could live with it for a long time with few symptoms beyond the tingling, for which there was medication.

In preparation for our walk across England, Trevor did little to prepare. We knew we would have to walk between 10-15 miles per day from one hostel or B&B to the next, but the thought didn't deter him. His primary-care physician left it up to Trevor to take this journey with no caveats or advice.

I was perhaps in slightly better shape since I regularly walked the dog, but I certainly wasn't a 15-mile-a-day walker. What were we thinking? Our imaginations were stronger than our lungs and leg muscles.

That first day, we kept thinking, It must be five miles now, then, I'm sure we've gone ten. When we finally reached our accommodations after 14 or 15 miles, we could hardly make it up the stairs. We collapsed on the bed, more exhausted than I'd ever felt. There was a pub nearby where we could get dinner, and I ventured over, barely able to move. The fact that Trevor couldn't accompany me—a pub aficionado who never passed up a pint—showed just how exhausted he was. Eventually, he made his way there, but I could tell this walk was more than he had bargained for. We learned about buses that traveled the route and decided to ride part way, walking only the more scenic sections in smaller increments.

How do you know your capacity for physical challenges unless you try them? On this adventure, I learned something Trevor had worked hard to conceal— he was much more physically diminished than he would ever admit. His capacity for denial was notable. He became easily fatigued and quite wobbly but would get angry if I showed concern. I found myself working around this denial creatively. If I knew he needed to rest but wouldn't admit it, I would say I needed a break or a snack or water.

This dance of his denials and my "workarounds" became the theme of his long, slow decline from 2007 until December 2019, when denial would no longer work. He couldn't walk and could barely lift himself from bed. When offered Hospice care, he resignedly agreed without argument, making a joke of it by calling the Hospice staff "dead enders."

But here is where the grief trigger took hold of me. As I walked down that tree-rutted, half-frozen path in New Hampshire, I had a flashback of Trevor walking so unsteadily along Hadrian's Wall. He was leaning as if the tumor in his brain was pulling him forward, making his way almost comically down that path. I offered help, but he rebuffed me, insisting he was fine—his way of preserving pride and denying his decline.

When my grandson offered the advice to lean back while walking downhill, I was transported to that day of hiking with Trevor, unsteadily leaning and wobbling. I let the tears fall, for him, and for me.

These grief triggers, I've learned, are an integral part of the journey through loss. They come unexpectedly—in a grandson's innocent advice, in the way sunlight filters through trees just as it did on a long-ago walk, in the sound of laughter from a nearby pub. They're not always painful: sometimes they bring a bittersweet smile, a warm memory, a moment of connection with what has been lost. I've stopped trying to avoid them or brace myself against them. Instead I've come to understand that they are love's echo, resonating through time, keeping Trevor's memory alive in the most ordinary moments of my days.

Like the mountain paths and the wooded trails I still walk, grief isn't a straight line from loss to healing. It winds and doubles back, sometimes steep, sometimes gentle, but always leading somewhere. These triggers are the cairns along the trail, marking places where memory and present moment meet. They remind me that great love leaves an indelible mark on our hearts, and that even in absence, that love continues to shape our journey forward, one step at a time.

Grief Visits

Grief visits again
> she steals my joy

disturbs my
> equilibrium

Some days she leaves
> me alone
To wander the place
> of hope

Then, unexpectedly
> she returns
and opens those wounds
> again, wide open
Will the wounds ever heal?

> I still walk with a limp

S. VandenBrink

What's lost is nothing to what's found; all the death that ever was set next to life, would scarcely fill a cup.

Frederick Buechner

"If we do not transform our pain, we will most surely transmit it."

Father Richard Rohr

Death Cleaning

I stood in the middle of my living room, feet planted, tears running down my face, as I scanned the room. My heart was heavy as I assessed the years of accumulated treasures—books, antiques, and family heirlooms scattered throughout. This was no longer a family home. It was no longer a "couple" home. I was the lone survivor of this establishment. My husband had died. My daughter and her family lived 800 miles away, and my stepchildren lived on the other side of the state. The house was empty except for the detritus of middle-class life: furniture, pictures, things saved and collected. It was just me, the house, and the "stuff."

An overwhelming sense of hollowness came over me. The walls echoed with memories as I stood in pained silence. I needed to make decisions, but not now, not today.

The living room, only a few weeks ago, was filled with a hospital bed, tray table, and miscellaneous medical equipment needed to care for my dying husband. Now, the room was back in order, all equipment moved expeditiously by Hospice. In fact, they remove all medical equipment within 24 hours. Swiftly removing the instruments of caregiving must seem like a humane gesture. And I suppose it is. But after 14 months of having our living room overtaken by medical equipment, it all seemed too empty and lonely.

The days, weeks, and months after Trevor's death were fraught with decisions that had to be made. There is the initial paperwork after a death. I remember little of this, on autopilot I suppose. Notify the bank, Social Security, the lawyers, make copies of the death certificate, cancel credit cards. I don't remember all of it. I'm quite sure Hospice gave me a list of things to do after the death. I scarcely recall doing them, yet I'm sure all tasks were completed even in my state of numbness.

My usual reaction to any kind of crisis or challenge is to take action. I found it difficult to simply live in that liminal space, directionless, waiting for what? Just to sit idle in my grief? I felt that I needed a plan in order to move ahead. Was it my desire to get over this painful episode? Throughout my life as I've struggled with depression, taking action was the best antidote.

What was to be my next move? The death and dying experts advise not to make any major decisions in the first year following the death of a spouse. Yet I felt ready to do something, to make a plan, to face the inevitable realization that everything was now left up to me. Oh, I could ask advice of my children or friends, but I knew that the decisions had to be mine.

My first decision was to find a worthy recipient of Trevor's clothing, shoes, and coats. I was especially interested in and supportive of the clothing ministry run by my church, St. John's Episcopal Church. The church had a partnership with an inner-city Episcopal congregation in an economically depressed area of Flint, Michigan. Members of my church traveled to Flint monthly to prepare a meal and distribute clothing to the homeless who gathered in the church for warmth and sustenance. Coincidentally, Trevor had started his career in social work in the city of Flint, a city that has experienced enormous hardship. I loaded up my car with a closet full of shirts, trousers, sweaters, shoes, boots, and heavy winter coats and dropped them off at the clothing bank. I knew Trevor would be pleased that his clothes were donated to men who struggled economically in the city where he had worked so hard to bring hope and healing in his profession as a social worker.

I was alone and feeling the burden of a house and possessions that no longer held meaning for me without the man who I adored and with whom we had created and curated a good life. What does one do with a lifetime of accumulated goods when the life that these possessions were purchased for no longer exists? Everything had shifted, nothing felt the same. Oh, the family pictures, the treasured family heirlooms, still held value. But so many of the other possessions felt as if their value had been diminished and their purpose and function no longer resonated. Everything felt hollow and empty, a stark reminder that my life as a spouse was over. Why did I need all these possessions as a person alone?

During that time of discerning my future plans and the new life ahead of me, I entertained many thoughts. I would sell everything, buy a van and travel throughout the United States. I considered moving to England to be closer to Trevor's sisters. Maybe I should move closer to my children? That did not seem like a good choice since they were not settled or certain how long they would be staying in New England. I was really at a place where I could have moved anywhere, and I did give this an enormous amount of thought. In my moments of greatest despair, I considered simply running away with no destination in mind, but that, I knew, was a reaction to my sense of being lost, unmoored.

Still I wrestled with decisions about my home and my accumulated possessions. I became somewhat obsessed with sorting and making decisions about what to keep and what to get rid of. I had read articles that declared, "your children don't want your stuff." I knew this to be true and there were only a few sentimental items that our children would take.

I had read about Swedish Death Cleaning and decided it was something I should consider. The name sounds morbid, but it is actually a practice that all older people should follow. The idea is that you will purge your possessions and organize your belongings so your children are not burdened with your various collections and pieces of which they have no interest.

I have always been a bit of a minimalist, but as I looked around my home realizing that I was now alone with a house, a garage, and a storage shed full of "stuff," I decided that I would take action. My possessions felt like a burden. I was weighed down with grief, but now it occurred to me that I was weighed down by possessions. Everything in my life had shifted, altered. I was alone in a house full of furniture and furnishings that I really did not want. I had the feeling that these things were a tether, tying me to a life that didn't exist anymore.

I spent a lifetime consuming, collecting, curating our home and lives into the dream we had of the life we wanted. I had read design magazines to get ideas for decorating our family home. Like many people, we had our own "collectibles" and cabinets to display them. Our home was full of souvenirs collected on our many travels and treasured reminders of our vacations. And yet, my husband's death reminded me that when we come to the end of our lives, we must let go of things. Our family had spent years accumulating possessions; now it was time to decide what I needed to let go of.

Death is a great awakening; it sharpens our sense of reality, of what is truly important in life. I was doing a personal inventory of my life, trying to discern how I wanted to live the remainder of my time on this earth. I was beginning to detach from things and realizing that what I wanted was people, experiences, the opportunity to give of myself for the greater good. I knew I did not want to be burdened by possessions.

Trevor's death left me feeling broken and untethered. Yet I knew that I must carry on, to find a way to redeem my grief and loss. I found strength in my faith in a God who I believed was as close as my breath. I claimed the words of Isaiah 41:10, "Fear not, for I am with you; be not dismayed, for I am your God; I will strengthen you, I will help you, I will uphold you with my righteous right hand."

In the end, I sold most of my possessions, sold my home, and bought a condominium that would free me from endless chores. Then a year and a half after Trevor's death, I received a call to return to serve the church I had retired from. I felt unburdened and ready to serve God even though my heart was still grieving.

It is astonishing to consider the ways that God works in and through each of us who remain open to God's guidance. My grief is still with me, but the burden of grief is not as heavy.

I'm grateful that I took a year to make decisions about my new life, my possessions, and the place to which God was calling me. It felt risky, and yet in some ways it felt empowering.

Proverbs 3:5-6 were words that I could claim:

> Trust in the Lord with all your heart; and lean not on your own understanding. In all your ways acknowledge God and he will direct your path.

"The reality is that you will grieve forever. You will not 'get over' the loss of a loved one; you will learn to live with it. You will heal and you will rebuild yourself around the loss you have suffered. You will be whole again but you will never be the same. Nor should you be the same, nor would you want to."

Elizabeth Kubler Ross

Rugby days

St. Nicholas Parish Church
Hornsea
East Yorkshire

Noel Trevor Matthews
1938 - 2021

Saturday 17th December 2022
10 a.m.

Memorial Service held in Hornsea in the church where
Trevor sang in the Boys Choir as a child.

Scattering the ashes at the North Sea Beach in Hornsea
where Trevor spent part of this childhood.

Chloe and Avery scattering the ashes.

Stewarding Our Pain

The plane was small and narrow-bodied, and I was one of the last to board. As the first leg of a long journey to Alaska, I didn't mind getting a bad seat. It would be a short flight to my next destination. I struggled with my two overstuffed carry-on bags, clumsily making my way up the aisle while trying not to bump anyone. My seat was in the very last row—an aisle seat next to a man who was obviously too large for his space. I knew I would need to pull in my arms, making myself as small as possible. The man kindly smiled and greeted me with a knowing chuckle at my misfortune. After wedging my rolling suitcase into the overhead bin, I gingerly settled into my seat, remaining quiet for the rest of the trip, wondering if I had made the right decision.

This was my first trip to Alaska, flying solo, as I had several times in the three years since my husband's death. My fears weren't about the flight, or traveling alone—they stemmed from what lay ahead. I had enrolled in a week-long writers' retreat called Your Story Matters, where I would embark on a journey of self-reflection, facing my past to learn its secrets and lessons. I knew that writing about my time as my husband's caregiver and his death after a long illness would reopen wounds that had begun to heal. Or so I thought.

I had requested a single room at the retreat, held in the home of our retreat leader, Leslie Leyland Fields, a renowned writer and creative writing teacher. Leslie's home on Kodiak Island was built upon a rocky outcropping with a breathtaking ocean view. Each day brought new delights: seabirds soaring overhead, dolphins and whales emerging from the depths—a feast for the senses. I knew that in this place of incredible natural beauty, I would need time alone for quiet reflection. While the teaching of writing involves skill-building, the internal process of delving into memories requires a deep dive into times, places, and people fraught with both joy and sorrow. These memories needed to be explored and mined for their profound impact on my life and the choices I would make for the future.

The writer Frederick Buechner wrote about the profound effect his father's suicide had on his life. Though Buechner was just a young boy when it happened, the tragedy shaped his path in unexpected ways. He became a pastor and an incredibly gifted writer whose deep insights have challenged and comforted many people through their own struggles. It was observed of him, and he came to embrace the idea, that he had become a "good steward of his pain." Though his father's suicide left a deep wound, he transformed that painful experience into something meaningful—using it for insight and the care of others who struggle.

I knew that attending the writers' retreat meant opening wounds that might have been easier to leave alone, to scab over and neglect in the past. But as painful as it might be, I needed to examine the events of my husband's long illness and death to gain new insights, develop a deeper perspective, and discern how to move forward in my grief, transforming my pain into a source of hope for myself and others.

Writing about memories and life events has become somewhat of an obsession. I've learned that in writing our stories, there is both an outer story and an inner story. The outer story involves retelling events as factually as memory allows, requiring us to revisit places and times that may have been painful or confusing. But in the retelling, we reflect on lessons learned, mining for nuggets of wisdom and deeper understanding—this is our inner story. And in that mining we may find amazing treasures that transform our lives.

Writing our stories can have a profound healing effect. Delving into our pain isn't easy, and we may prefer to divert our eyes, switch off those painful memories, and move on. But most psychological counselors will tell you that unaddressed pain and trauma can become buried in our minds, potentially emerging later as physical illnesses or addictions. Facing our pain means talking about it, writing about it, and yes, spending time in prayer and meditation.

Through the process of "working" with grief and loss, you eventually discover that you are stronger and more capable than you imagined. While you will always grieve, you reach a point where your wounded self becomes capable of helping others. On Kodiak Island, I learned that I could mine my grief for lessons and opportunities to use my pain to help others. Armed with greater sensitivity and empathy, we are at our strongest point to be of service.

The path of stewarding our pain isn't a straight line but a spiral, moving us through familiar territory at deeper levels.

Each time we return to our stories—whether through writing, sharing, or quiet reflection—we discover new insights. On Kodiak Island, surrounded by the raw beauty of nature and the gentle support of fellow writers, I learned that pain can be transformed without being diminished. Now, when I meet others facing similar journeys, I share what I've learned: keep a journal; join a writing group; seek out beauty in unexpected places; find a kind, listening ear, whether a friend or a professional counselor. There is no shame in seeking help through your grief journey. Wise professionals helped me gain perspective and strength in some of my darkest times. Kind friends were generous in their time and willingness to listen at some of my most tearful moments. Most importantly, remain open to the possibility that your deepest wounds, when carefully tended, can become wellsprings of connection and healing. In the end, stewarding our pain isn't just about managing our own grief—it's about creating safe harbors where others can anchor their own stories of loss and transformation.

"Trauma is not just an event that took place sometime in the past; it is also the imprint left by that experience on mind, brain, and body."

Dr. Bessel van der Kolk

"The voice of God calling
upon the people to weep,
lament, and mourn, for
the calamities are about
to descend upon them,
is itself a voice of grief,
a voice of weeping."

Abraham Joshua Heschel

Acknowledgments

I didn't intend to write a memoir about my grief and healing journey. I was inspired at a Writers' Retreat on Kodiak Island, Alaska. Your Story Matters Memoir Writing Program, designed and facilitated by award-winning author, speaker, and educator, Leslie Leyland Fields, was the nudge I needed to write my story. Story writing has become a deeply meaningful and healing experience. I'm so grateful for Leslie's inspiration!

Furthermore, I've had editorial guidance from author and friend Steve Dieleman, who offered expert editorial advice and encouraged me every step of the way. Friends who generously read my drafts and gave amazing feedback and encouragement include Lori Van Doornink, Judith Effa Ford, Dianne Mishra, and Karin Orr. Innumerable others encouraged me, and through these recent months have listened to my story. I'm so grateful for the time they invested in helping me offer a clear manuscript and narrative flow.

I will be forever grateful to Hospice of Mid-Michigan, and especially our dedicated caregiver, Kathy Kemp, who so lovingly and gently cared for Trevor.

I would not have survived the heartbreak of grief and loss without the support of my children and grandchildren, who visited Trevor and lifted his spirits, and gave me a shoulder to cry on, and encouragement for those long, lonely days going solo. Thank you, Robert, Dianne, Alok, Finley, Meghana, Chloe, J.T., and Avery. I love you all more than you could ever know.

Through my experience of grief and healing, I was carried by the God who "became flesh and blood, and moved into the neighborhood" (Peterson, The Message, John 1)

Being lifted up and comforted by a Savior who suffered and knew the depths of grief, and understood me completely, gave me the strength to go on in my darkest times. For that I am eternally grateful.

Additional Resources

Leslie Leyland Fields, *Your Story Matters* (NavPress 2020).

Jeffrey Munroe, *Telling Stories in the Dark* (Reformed Journal Books 2024).

Nicholas Wolterstorff, *Lament for a Son* (WmEerdmans 1987).

Alan D. Wolfelt PhD, *Understanding Your Grief* (Companion Press 2003).

Francis Weller, *The Wild Edge of Sorrow* (North Atlantic Books 2015).

Alan D. Wolfelt, *Companioning the Bereaved* (Companion Press 2006).

Leslie Leyland Fields, *Nearing a Far God* (NavPress 2024).

Bessel Van der Kolk *The Body Keeps the Score* (Penguin Books 2014).

C.S. Lewis, *A Grief Observed* (Seabury Press, 1961).

Kate Bowler, *Everything Happens for a Reason: and Other Lies I've Loved* (Random House, 2018).

Frederick Buechner, *Telling Secrets: A Memoir* (HarperSanFrancisco,1991).

Writing Prompts
for Further Reflection

Looking back, what were some of the challenging times around the death of your loved one?

What are the most vivid memories you have of your loved one's passing?

Was there a time when you realized that despite your grief you knew you would be all right and that you were on the road to healing?

How has your grief changed you?

What are your fears about moving forward?

The Author

Sandra VandenBrink

I am a retired United Methodist pastor, and have been a
psychotherapist in private practice, a Hospice chaplain,
and a trained end of life doula. I cared for my sick and
dying husband and have walked the long and lonely path
of grief. Through those days of grieving the loss of my
beloved husband, my sister, and mother, along with so
many parishioners and hospice patients, I have learned
that grief is work. Grief is painful, lonely, and an enormous
adjustment in one's life, health, and overall well-being.
Research has shown that grief changes us, even changes
our brains. Grief is a type of trauma that all of us will
experience. Death is something which we are loath to talk
about, anticipate, or face. Until we must. Then we are ill
equipped to walk that road of loss and mourning. Most of
us would rather ignore it, get on with our lives.

It is my mission to help others face death, mourning and
grief so that it can be gentle and meaningful, so one can
work through it and come out the other side stronger, more

resilient, wiser, and more empathetic. We can do it, and in doing grief well we can be a blessing to others. If we bury our grief and don't find ways to redeem it or grow from it, we will be diminished in some way, by depression, physical illness, or an inability to form and nurture other relationships.

In my stories of grief, and through this journey of caring for my dying husband, I pray you will find encouragement and a desire to think more deeply about your grief and loss, and find even a small amount of blessing in it. And more, I pray you emerge from the darkest days of grief to be able to say that you can see life more clearly, deeply, and full of possibility for a brighter future.

Shalom